ASIAN LAW SERIES

School of Law

University of Washington

Number 16

The Asian Law Series was initiated in 1969,
with the cooperation of the University of Washington Press
and the Institute for Comparative and Foreign Area Studies
(now the Henry M. Jackson School of International Studies),
in order to publish the results of several projects under way
in Japanese, Chinese, and Korean law.
The members of the editorial committee are
Jere L. Bacharach, Donald C. Clarke, Toshiko Takenaka,
and Veronica L. Taylor (chair).

ASIAN LAW SERIES
School of Law
University of Washington

ANTITRUST

in Germany and Japan

The First Fifty Years, 1947–1998

JOHN O. HALEY

UNIVERSITY OF WASHINGTON PRESS

Seattle and London

Library of Congress Cataloging-in-Publication Data
Haley, John Owen.
Antitrust in Germany and Japan : the first fifty years, 1947–1998 / John O. Haley.
p.   cm. — (Asian law series ; no. 16)
Includes bibliographical references and index.
ISBN 0-295-97987-9 (alk. paper)
1. Antitrust law—Germany—History.
2. Antitrust law—Japan—History.
I. Title. II. Series.
K3850.H35   2000   343.43'0721—DC21   00-033789

The paper used in this publication is acid free and recycled from 10 percent
post-consumer and at least 50 percent pre-consumer waste. It meets the
minimum requirements of American National Standard for Information
Sciences—Permanence of Paper for Printed Library Materials,
ANSI Z39.48–1984. ☉ ⊛

To Griffith Way

Contents

CONTENTS

Preface

Since World War II, antitrust legislation of some sort has been enacted in more than eighty countries, from Argentina to Zaire. In this proliferation of national antitrust legislation over the past half century, the antitrust statutes of Germany and Japan have acquired senior status. The year 1997 marked the end in each country of a half century of experience with antitrust regulation. Fittingly, just as the second half century began, major amendments in both countries have ushered in a new era. Outside of the United States, Germany and Japan have thus had the longest and, judging by recent legislation in Europe and Asia, most influential antitrust regimes in the world. That experience and the patterns they have established are likely to continue to rival American antitrust influence. We need to know about both.

Despite important similarities in the antitrust legislation in the two countries and, in the case of Japan, significant borrowing from the other, the abundant literature in English on each is bereft of any comparative study. This work is intended to fill the gap.

We begin in part 1 with a historical survey of the origins and development of antitrust legislation in the two countries. The story of the American origins through 1947, detailed in chapter 1, is rich in irony. More important are the lessons to be learned from the errors made and their consequences. Chapter 2 continues this history with a summary of the vicissitudes in the development of antitrust policy in both from 1948 through 1998. Particular emphasis is placed on the extent to which antitrust policy and its enforcement in the two countries initially tended for various reasons to converge. Despite contrasts that have emerged and become more pronounced during the past decade, the antitrust regimes in Germany and Japan remain considerably more alike than either the original statutes or their early history would suggest.

We turn in part 2 to an equally neglected aspect of antitrust law: enforcement. Here the treatment of the two laws is less historical and more technical. The first chapter (chapter 3) compares the substantive provisions of the two statutes in detail. Also included is a comparative overview of their enforcement during the past fifty years. The focus shifts in chapter 4 to the institutions and procedures of enforcement, the most disparate aspects of the two laws. In chapter 5 we turn to remedies and sanctions, another area of considerable contrasts in statutory provisions, yet similarities in practice, and, at least by the Japanese, borrowing.

Part 2 deserves particular emphasis. Much of the reality of any regulatory scheme lies in the processes of enforcement and sanctions. Living law is enforced law. To treat substantive provisions of any statute without an accurate appreciation of means and extent of its formal and informal enforcement is a most rarified exercise. For the comparativist in particular, much is gained by examining the process of law enforcement. Only by doing so can one discern the crucial features of a dynamic legal process.

The study concludes with an assessment. Despite the insurmountable hurdles to any accurate measure of either the success or failure of antitrust in any country, at least one conclusion can be made with reasonable certainty. In both Germany and Japan antitrust regulation has had a significant educational effect. Public tolerance of what might be called "core" antitrust violations such as price fixing, bid rigging, and group boycotts has decreased. This change in public attitudes may be the most significant contribution of the half century of antitrust in both Germany and Japan.

Acknowledgments

The research on German law for this study began in the Federal Republic of Germany in 1981 at the Institute for Economic Law, Labor, and Social Insurance Law of the Albert-Ludwigs University in Freiburg in Breisgau under the auspices of the Alexander von Humboldt Foundation. I have thus long been indebted to Professor Dr. Fritz Rittner and Klaus Blemer for their patient help in guiding me through the intricacies of German law and correcting so many of my initial errors. The research on German law was supplemented during the summer of 1997 with the generous support of the Max Planck Institute for Foreign and International Private Law in Hamburg. I am particularly grateful to Dr. Harald Baum for his many kindnesses as my host. My indebtedness during this visit also extends to others. Dr. Hansjürgen Ruppelt of the Federal Cartel Office, then located in Berlin, and Professor Dr. Ernst-Joachim Mestmäcker, former director of the Max Planck Institute in Hamburg, were especially generous with their time helping to clarify details and to answer questions related to German enforcement practice and the history of antitrust in Germany.

My study of Japanese antitrust law began while working with the law firm of Blakemore and Mitsuki in Tokyo in the early 1970s. After joining the faculty of the University of Washington School of Law in 1974, I developed the first course on Japanese antitrust law taught regularly outside Japan. Professor Mitsuo Matsushita, at that time professor of law at Sophia University and subsequently at the University of Tokyo, and I taught together and collaborated on the materials for this course in Seattle during the summer of 1978 and at Monash University in Melbourne, Australia, in 1980. I also made several research trips to Japan, the first of which was also in 1980 with support from the Toyota Foundation.

A note of special appreciation is owed to Professor Akira Shōda of Keio University, who pioneered the comparative study of German and Japanese antitrust law, as well as three other close friends in Japan: former secretary general and commissioner of the Japanese Fair Trade Commission, Hiroshi Iyori; Hideto Ishida, a former member of the FTC staff and currently partner of the Anderson and Mori law firm in Tokyo; and Professor Kenji Sanekata of Hokkaido University, whose assistance and comments have always been invaluable.

I have also been fortunate to have two friends and colleagues in Seattle who have consistently given me good advice and direction over the duration of this effort. Each reviewed early drafts and provided insightful counsel. To each—Professor Kozo Yamamura and Dr. Eleanor Hadley—I owe a special debt that will be difficult to repay.

Much of my research on the history of antitrust in Germany and Japan reflects the support of Mary Whisner, Nancy McMurrer, Cheryl Nyberg, John Holcolm, and other reference librarians of the Marian Gallagher Law Library of the University of Washington, whose dedication is surpassed only by their skills. Similarly, the research on Japanese antitrust law would not have been possible without the extraordinary collection of materials available in the East Asian Law Department and the assistance of its capable staff, William McCloy and Robert Britt.

Joachim Rudo, a visiting scholar at the University of Washington School of Law in 1998–99, painstakingly ferreted out many errors and suggested nearly as many areas for improvement. My secretary, Jean Knight, and Joanne Sandstrom, who edited the final manuscript, each spent many, many hours on the manuscript. Finally, I also thank the three unnamed readers who reviewed the manuscript for the University of Washington Press.

Despite the all of the advice I have received over many years, errors remain. They are, I hasten to note, entirely mine.

An early version of the historical comparison of the origins and development of antitrust policy in Germany and Japan in chapter two was first presented at the conference "The Political Management of the Economy in Post Germany and Japan," held in Ito, Japan, in September 1982. It was subsequently expanded into an article published in 1998 as an essay titled "Error, Irony and Convergence: A Comparative Study of the Origins and Development of German and Japanese Law," in *Festschrift für Wolfgang Fikentscher,* edited by

Bernhard Großfeld, Rolf Sack, Thomas M. J. Möllers, Josef Drexl, and Andreas Heinemann (Munich: C. H. Beck, 1998; pp. 876–918). The final chapter was first published as "Antitrust Sanctions and Remedies: A Comparative Study of German and Japanese Law," *Washington Law Review,* vol. 59, no. 3 (1984), pp. 471–508. It has been revised and included here with permission.

ANTITRUST

in Germany and Japan

PART 1

THE ORIGINS AND DEVELOPMENT
OF ANTITRUST LEGISLATION IN
GERMANY AND JAPAN

The historical contexts out of which antitrust policy developed in the Federal Republic of Germany and Japan appear in many respects to be similar. Both countries had much in common as rapidly developing "follower" states playing industrial catch-up to Great Britain in the late nineteenth and early twentieth centuries. Both experienced an interwar democratic interval followed by the rise of a militaristic, collectivist state in the 1930s. And in both, antitrust policy was initially a product of military defeat, occupation, and American command.

Conventional wisdom also teaches that despite common points of departure and destination the two countries traveled along very different paths toward economic recovery during the postwar period. Germany chose competition, the free market, and European integration. Japan opted for pervasive governmental guidance, industrial policy, and trade protection. Antitrust policy in Germany is credited with success and is commonly viewed as a contributing factor in the German postwar economic miracle. In contrast, the Japanese economic miracle is attributed, paradoxically to some, to an industrial policy favoring concentration, cartels, and a vigorous market economy. Japan's postwar antitrust policy has been deemed by nearly all accounts a failure.

A closer look at the German and Japanese experiences suggests that such views err. At least with respect to antitrust policy, Germany and Japan had far less in common prior to World War II and much more thereafter. Significant differences separate the two countries. Competition policy in postwar Germany, for example, had strong indigenous intellectual and political support. Occupation legislation provided a critical catalyst, but few question the prevailing influence of the "ordo-liberals" of the Freiburg School and their most prominent political proponent, Ludwig Erhard, in forging an enduring competition policy for postwar Germany. Antitrust policy served to restrain corporatist tendencies first in Germany and then in Europe, demonstrating in turn the persuasive force of German law as a model for global emulation. Japan, in contrast, did not develop an internal intellectual basis for an economic policy to foster competition until much later. Any thought of competition policy in the immediate postwar period would in any event have been overwhelmed by prevailing Marxist and mercantilist paradigms. For nearly a quarter-century, antitrust law seemed an alien legacy of a lost war. Nobusuke Kishi as bureaucrat and politician represented the political and business leaders who feared "excessive competition" as a debilitating feature of an unmanaged economy. Not until the late 1960s did indigenous support for a strong antitrust regime begin to develop, ultimately ending a decade of neglect. Yet in the process, antitrust policy became increasingly embedded in economic law, establishing the limits of industrial policy and demonstrating again Japan's remarkable capacity for effective reception of ideas and legal institutions from abroad.

American policies and the attitudes and beliefs that motivated those who made them also deserve close comparative attention. American antitrust policy provided the impetus as well as a stumbling block for German and Japanese antitrust law. The initial emphasis was on political aims—demilitarization and democratization—as the primary justifications for antitrust at home as well as in both Germany and Japan. American efforts to eliminate cartels and economic concentrations thus left a strong if not indelible impression that antitrust policies were antithetical to economic recovery and growth. In the early postwar years no political leader—except Erhard—argued forcefully in positive terms that antitrust law and the competitive economic order it was intended to foster would have positive economic consequences. Erhard's postwar speeches and writings stand out today as among the most thoughtful and eloquent arguments for competition policy of all postwar policy makers and political leaders. Although Erhard and the ordo-liberals in Germany were able to overcome the perception that antitrust would lower production and slow growth, in Japan these views remained strong for more than a generation.

A focus on Nazi Germany dominated the making of American antitrust policy in Japan. Except for a small band of Japan specialists, Americans knew very little and seemed to care less about Japan before the war. Those engaged during the war in presurrender plans for occupied Germany and Japan thus tended to equate Japan with Germany and to ignore the differences that distinguished the two. Even the antitrust economists involved in planning American postwar international economic policies and who were instrumental in drafting the restrictive practices provisions of the Havana Charter tended to justify their objectives in public in terms of the Nazi experience. They virtually ignored Japan. As the war ended, U.S. policy for Germany was simply adopted with slight modifications for Japan. The influence of American policies in Germany on Japan continued during the occupation.

Nor was the "reverse course" a purely Japanese or Asian affair. The key figure in the termination of the *zaibatsu* dissolution program in Japan was General William H. Draper, Jr. As head of the Economic Division under the Office of the Military Governor of the United States (OMGUS) in Germany, Draper believed that radical deconcentration was a detriment to efforts to assist German economic recovery. Later, as undersecretary of the army, Draper successfully opposed the extended *zaibatsu* dissolution program in Japan.

The parallels between American policy in Germany and Japan do not end here. Almost as soon as the implementation of American policies began in both countries, they were the focus of fierce American political controversy. The debates pitted Marxist progressives against conservative and liberal elites. Liberal Democrats railed against the occupation authorities in Germany for not doing enough. Conservative Republicans vilified the American reformers in Japan for doing too much. Readers of a Manichean bent may choose their particular villains and heroes at will.

Lost in the debates—even as they echo today—however, were the parameters of agreement. All sides tacitly acquiesced in the premises that cartels and economic concentrations were political evils but also that antitrust—at least as imposed on Germany and Japan—would slow economic recovery. Deconcentration in Germany and *zaibatsu* dissolution in Japan were depicted as restraints on economic growth and future prosperity, well-meaning at best and retributive at worst. No wonder then that the prevailing American attitudes retarded public support for competition policy as a means to invigorate the economy and to promote innovation and industrial expansion in both Germany and Japan.

The gap that separated those who actively engaged in the controversies was narrow. Americans on both sides agreed on the basics. Hardly any one, left or right, affirmed cartels or monopoly. Unlike British, German, and Japanese socialists, the American left—except the most extreme[1]—did not view industrial concentration as an inexorable or useful prelude to a nationalized economy. Nor did those on the right—however pro-business they may have seemed—agree with German industrialists that concentration rather than competition was a natural or necessary prerequisite for industrial growth or that government should play no role in preserving a competitive economic order. Viewed in a broader, more global context, these controversies seem peculiarly American, quaintly naive responses to the intellectual battles between the two totalitarian ideologies that had engulfed Europe in the 1930s. All the same, they had an unfortunate effect on German and Japanese attitudes toward antitrust.

The controversies shared similar origins but, like a play acted out by very different troupes in separate theaters, they diverged, each a mirror image of the other. In the opening scenes, a single actor—Draper—played in both. Two generals had the leading roles as the military commanders of their respective theaters. Both West Point graduates and career military officers, one, Lucius Clay, a lifelong Democrat and son of a populist Georgia senator, would lead the "reverse course" and curtail the deconcentration program in Germany. The other, Douglas MacArthur, the Republican who sought his party's nomination to become president, would resist the critics and defend the actions of the "New Deal trustbusters" in Japan until at last compelled by superiors to yield.

No actors were more central to the drama or to how the play was subsequently to unfold, however, than Erhard and Kishi. Both rose in concomitant sequence and timing to positions of official influence and power as economic ministers and later heads of government in postwar Germany and Japan. Both owed their careers in part to occupation policies and structure. Competition for Erhard, the antitrust advocate, was the heartbeat of German economic well-being, but for Kishi, an architect of Japan's industrial policy, it was a threatening menace to economic recovery and growth.

Despite these contrasts and controversies, once in place the antitrust policies of the two countries began gradually to converge. In Japan, German law provided the principal model for reform, first to weaken and then to strengthen the law. A similar pattern of change albeit more slowly also occurred in Germany as features common to both American and Japanese law were incorporated while the patterns of enforcement and exemptions tended over time to coincide with Japan's. In short, the story of antitrust in Germany and Japan is one of error, irony, remarkable transformation, and, at least until the last decade of our story, considerably more convergence than most observers acknowledge.

1 / Error and Irony—the American Impetus

From the late nineteenth century through the early 1930s, Germany and Japan shared much in common as newly arrived industrial and military powers, each with formidable continental rivals. In government and law the similarities were equally pronounced. Japan had looked primarily to Germany for its constitutional and basic legal institutions. At the turn of the century Japan turned to German codes and legal theory for emulation. Nevertheless, the contrasts in industrial organization and structure between Germany and Japan overshadowed any similarities of context or direction. The foundations of antitrust policy were as different as they could be.

FOUNDATIONS

Following the economic recession of the mid 1870s, Germany abandoned free trade and laissez-faire as the foundational principles of economic policy in favor of a more protectionist role for the state. Private law—and with it, the principles of private autonomy and freedom of contract—still prevailed, however, as the primary source of legal regulation. As a result, the inherent conflict of legal principles between the freedom of producers to contract to set prices or restrict production and the explicit constraints such agreements placed on their buyers' autonomy in the market could not be avoided. Early cases, beginning with a decision by the Bavarian High Court in 1888[2] and culminating in the Reichsgericht's decision in the 1897 wood products cartel case,[3] allowed the private regulation of markets by contract. The courts in effect viewed col-

7

lective self-regulation of prices by an industry as a normal and reasonable response by the "nature of things" (*Natur der Sache*) to overproduction. So too was concentration. By merger and acquisition, major German enterprises in steel and chemicals established large, vertically integrated conglomerates.

By the mid 1920s cartels—that is, agreements or other arrangements among competitors to restrict prices, output, and other forms of competition—had become so characteristic of German industrial life that Germany is frequently described as the fatherland of the cartel movement.[4] Aside from minor disputes over the exact number, few disagree that cartel arrangements increased at a rapid pace from the turn of the century. By the eve of mandatory cartel legislation in the mid 1930s under the National Socialist regime, all significant segments of German industry were subject to some form of private price and output regulation. Heinz Müller and Gerhard Gries[5] estimate that, although in 1875 there were only eight cartels in Germany, by 1905 the numbers had grown to 2,000 and by 1935 there were 2,250 cartels affecting 1,700 industries. The Weimar Republic did attempt some degree of regulation under the Cartel Decree (*Kartellverordnung*) of 1923,[6] but the cartel court it established is credited for having been more effectual in enforcing cartel agreements than policing abuses.[7] From regulation by private cartelization, it was an easy step to government-sponsored cartel organizations, the pattern adopted under the Third Reich.

The cartel movement was not a uniquely German phenomenon. Voluntary cartels and government marketing restrictions proliferated in almost all industrial countries during the interwar period. As described by Stocking and Watkins, "Between World Wars I and II producers everywhere sought to escape the risks and uncertainties of competition. They were no longer content to rely on self-help in a competitive struggle with business rivals. To ease the rigors of the competition and promote group welfare they turned with increasing frequency to cartel arrangements."[8]

During this period government-sponsored international and voluntary cartels covered a vast array of products. Through patent pools, territorial restrictions, and agreements not to compete, by the early 1930s a high proportion of all major manufactures and basic industrial commodities had become subject to price-fixing or output-restraining agreements. Few agricultural products, minerals, or chemicals escaped restriction. By 1939 in the United States, for example—well after the demise of the New Deal's initial experiment with an "industrial policy" of cartelization under the National Industrial Recovery Act (NIRA)—an estimated 47.4 percent by value of all agricultural products and 86.9 percent of all minerals produced are estimated to have been subject to cartel restrictions.[9]

Japan was more victim than player in the interwar cartel movement. Dependent upon imports for nearly all foodstuffs, chemical fertilizers, minerals, oil, and other raw materials, Japanese consumers were forced to buy from the most successful international cartels. Japanese producers for export sold in the most competitive world markets. In a study of international cartels in existence in 1939, Heinrich Kronstein listed 215 cartel agreements covering 172 separate manufactures and commodities.[10] German firms participated in 137, followed in number by 88 U.S. firms and 84 U.K. firms. Only a dozen related to Japan or had any Japanese participation.

The most closely studied international cartels that involved Japanese producers reveal a telling pattern—the more effective the cartel in restraining price competition in the Japanese market, the greater the acceleration of production capacity by nonparticipating Japanese firms. Except in response to sustained predatory dumping into the Japanese market or otherwise to control imports, Japanese producers rarely joined international cartels. Their net effect with respect to Japan was to create incentives and opportunities for Japanese firms to expand and thereby to intensify competition within Japanese domestic markets as well as Japan's principal export markets.[11]

In contrast to Germany and the other industrial nations during this period, the Japanese economy continued to be characterized by fierce firm rivalry despite the development of the conglomerate industrial and financial combines known as the *zaibatsu* and a similar increase in cartel-like arrangements. Japan had relatively few successful—that is, effectively restrictive—voluntary industrial cartels or restrictive industrial associations until the 1930s. Even after 1931, government-mandated cartels did not effectively contain firm rivalry. New entrants, even the creation of new *zaibatsu,* were common except in banking and other sectors of the economy subject to government licensing controls.

To be sure, attempts were made in Japan to restrain competition. Yet there is little evidence that these were successful or significant.[12] The first trade associations were organized in the 1880s, beginning with the paper and textile industries, but apparently it was not until the turn of the century that those associations began any serious effort to restrict competition.[13] During the 1894–95 Sino-Japanese War and at various other times before World War I, voluntary cartels were similarly organized in the chemical fertilizer, cotton textile, and railroad manufacturing industries.[14] After World War I, voluntary cartels continued to be formed. But by and large, we are told, most were ineffectual and short-lived.[15] Those that did endure tended to foster rather than discourage competition by creating new or more efficient rivals.[16]

The number of voluntary cartel arrangements increased during the period immediately before and after World War I but were limited to only a few fields of commerce until the financial crisis of 1921.[17] Most were in export trades. Many reflected attempts to coordinate and regulate labor markets. Few dealt with prices or output. Seldom could Japanese cartels effectively enforce price and output restrictions or limit new entry. In the words of Ryōkichi Minobe, "They were quite 'loose.'"[18] The only significant exception appears to have been the cotton spinners who were able to exert temporary control over output and prices through their trade organization, the Great Japan Cotton-Spinning Association (Dai Nippon Bōseki Rengōkai). The aims and at least longer-term effects of the association are disputed.[19]

The Major Export Goods Trade Association Law of 1897,[20] the Major Products Trade Association Law of 1900,[21] and other legislative measures enacted by Meiji-period governments did facilitate the organization of trade associations and thus cartel-like mechanisms for anticompetitive restraints, but, indicative of Japan's contrast with Germany, a governmental decree of 1916 prohibited price fixing.[22] Other legislative measures, such as the Banking Law of 1927,[23] established licensing systems that effectively barred entry into a variety of fields, but positive state intervention to encourage cartels did not come until 1931, as the Great Depression peaked in Japan, with the enactment of the Major Industries Control Law,[24] ostensibly to aid small and medium enterprises. At that time, it is estimated, only twenty-four cartels were formed under the Control Law in Japan, most of which were inactive.[25] Four years later there were still only thirty-five compulsory and fourteen voluntary cartels and eighty trade associations, again mostly for exporters.[26]

More problematic is the question of the effect of the *zaibatsu* on competition during the prewar period. In most cases, the *zaibatsu* were family-dominated conglomerates with a holding company as the head organ controlling through stock ownership a constellation of subsidiary firms in assorted manufacturing industries, finance, international trade, and mining. Although the origins of many, especially the Big Four—Mitsui, Mitsubishi, Sumitomo, and Yasuda—can be traced to the Tokugawa (1603–1867) or early Meiji (1868–1911) periods, they emerged in modern corporate form in the latter Taisho era (1912–26).[27] By absorption of smaller failing companies from this period through the mid 1930s, the ten largest combines[28] acquired oligopolistic positions of 10 to 20 percent of market output in key areas of manufacturing, banking, and commerce.[29] The *zaibatsu* differed significantly from similar combines in the industrial West. Neither Mitsui nor Mitsubishi was a Krupp or I. G. Farben, dominating a single industry. As described by Eleanor M. Hadley, "In the West, combines have been built on one industry in a group of closely related industries, with a view to achieving a monopolistic position. It was not so in Japan. The older (and the larger) of Japan's combines were all conglomerates, only some were more conglomerate than others. The goal was not high-market occupancy of a few related markets, but oligopolistic positions running the gamut of the modern sector of the economy."[30]

Whether oligopoly was a "goal" as Hadley contends or the incidental consequence of expansion can be disputed. The central issue is whether the *zaibatsu* tended to collude explicitly or tacitly "live and let live" or whether they tended to remain competitive rivals. The evidence for either proposition is slim. Primarily on theoretical grounds Hadley accepts the prevailing view that they barred entry and were probably collusive.[31] With respect to collusion, the available evidence, however scant, supports the opposite conclusion. The most credible analyses of competition and concentration in Japan's prewar economy remain those of British economist George C. Allen.[32] A persistent proponent of antitrust legislation for Great Britain, Allen played an instrumental role in the process that culminated in the enactment of the Monopolies Act of 1948, the United Kingdom's first comprehensive antitrust legislation.[33]

Writing in 1940, Allen argued that despite the domination of *zaibatsu* firms in Japanese banking and commerce, represented by the combined influence of the banking and trading companies of the Big Four *zaibatsu*, Japanese industry remained highly competitive.[34] Two factors were crucial. The first was the prevalence of small-scale manufacturers, which as late as 1939 continued to account for a large proportion of Japan's total manufactures and, in the case of textiles, the bulk of Japanese exports.[35] Even in Japan's large-scale industries, the plants, Allen concluded, were smaller or less specialized than those of Japan's industrial peers.[36] With respect to *zaibatsu* firms, as late as 1940 Allen observed a prevailing rivalry that without government intervention precluded effective collusion.[37] In his words, "The vast mass of small scale enterprises both in the traditional trades and in those manufacturing Western style goods are not planned from a center. On the contrary, among most of them, competition is as fierce as it was in the heyday of competitive individualism in Great Britain. Even in the large scale industries where many kinds of combinations have been formed, great difficulty has been found in carrying out schemes for the regulation of competition, and only recently have effective controls been devised."[38]

Nor despite their dominance in finance and trade were *zaibatsu* firms Japan's most important prewar manufacturers. None of Japan's textile manufacturers were *zaibatsu* subsidiaries. The four dominant *zaibatsu* also did not share a role in many of the most significant new manufacturing ventures, particularly motor vehicle and auto parts production, which Ford, General Motors, and Dunlap had commenced in the 1920s to be superseded with strong government support from the early 1930s by Nissan, Toyota, and Bridgestone.[39] Indeed, the history of Nissan Motors reflects the successful efforts by Japan's revisionist economic bureaucrats to aid the creation of new *zaibatsu* conglomerates by preferential treatment in Japan's Asian colonies, especially the newly acquired territory in Manchuria, to offset the political influence of the Big Four.

The military was adamant that the *zaibatsu* firms not set foot in the territory. In charge of forging an "industrial policy" in Manchuria, Nobusuke Kishi, a rising star in the Ministry of Commerce and Industry, made the decision to exclude the principal *zaibatsu* and to give Gisuke Aikawa's Nippon Sangyō K. K. (Nissan) a near monopoly in all aspects of Manchurian commercial, financial, and industrial development.[40] Even the largest *zaibatsu* could not prevent or preclude such new entrants. And, as Allen observed, much of Japan's manufacturing remained in the hands of small firms, sufficiently competitive to discourage any *zaibatsu* entry.

The *zaibatsu* were indeed the object of virulent criticism and, in the early 1930s, violent attack by Japan's ultranationists within the military and the civilian bureaucracy. For both military and civilian "revisionists" the *zaibatsu* represented the decadence of Japanese liberalism and party politics. Japanese ultranationalism is widely understood today as a product of agrarian disaffection, which greatly affected an army of predominately rural volunteers and conscripts, as well as bureaucrats like Kishi. One the most prominent was Kiichirō Hiranuma, who as career prosecutor and ultranationalist politician had sought to professionalize the Japanese civil bureaucracy to serve a self-defined national purpose untouched by the corrupting influence of selfish private interests.[41] Whoever coined the term "money clique" (*zaibatsu*) to disparage Japan's financial and commercial establishment is just as likely to have been a right-wing ultranationalist as a left-wing progressive. In short, big business was as much an anathema to the military and civilian ultranationalists who led Japan in the 1930s toward war as to those on the extreme left.[42] Neither group was concerned with competition and free markets. Both viewed capitalists through statist and collectivist lens.

The critical constraint of competition in the Japanese economy in the intermediate prewar period was not concentration, cartelization, or collusion, but governmental controls and preferences. As indicated in occupation studies, before 1935 the *zaibatsu* did not show significant growth in either profits or assets.[43] During the war, as Allen predicted, the gains were spectacular. With easier access to important officials in economic ministries and dominant positions in the control organizations, big business in Japan profited handsomely through subsidies, preferential procurement orders, and favorable allocations of capital and raw materials. Suppression of competition was the consequence of wartime constraints on access to capital and raw materials, accompanied by growth of close personal and institutional ties between the economic ministries, especially between the Ministry of Commerce and Industry on one hand and the *zaibatsu* and other dominant enterprises and control associations on the other. By the end of World War II, Japan had established what Yukio Noguchi tellingly refers to as the "1940s system," a complex network of governmental and distribution controls that functioned through quasi-autonomous cooperatives, industry associations, and mandatory control organizations.[44]

As war approached, the German and Japanese experiences bore closer resemblance. Germany again provided a model although the trend toward government-mandated cartels had begun in Japan in 1931.

The introduction of mandatory cartels imposed by the Nazi authorities as a mechanism for wartime controls attracted both *zaibatsu* managers and government officials in Japan. The Japanese business community may not have welcomed state intervention in any form,[45] but mandatory cartels were less offensive than controls that are more direct. The use of control organizations and trade associations ensured a greater degree of business autonomy while preserving the prerogatives of the economic ministries, especially the Ministry of Commerce and Industry, from the military bureaucrats. The result was a level of disorganization and inefficiency that severely damaged Japan's war effort. Of more enduring importance, the pattern of Japanese wartime controls established a complex set of relationships between the principal players—*zaibatsu* middle managers and the economic bureaucrats.

As noted, the first systematic state intervention to encourage cartels did not come until the enactment of the 1931 Law concerning Control of Major Industries and the amendments[46] to the Major Export Goods Trade Association Law and Industrial Association Law. Full cartelization came only in 1937 on the eve of national mobilization (1938), as part of Japan's system of wartime economic controls. The operation of these controls is best summarized by economist Jerome B. Cohen:

> By 1940 a bewildering variety of government controls had been added to the already complex "autonomous" controls and cartel arrangements in all fields of industry. Small business was being squeezed out, but big business had not achieved complete control. The government, despite its numerous powers on the statute books, was not a cohesive, unifying directive force in the economic sphere. It was subject to pressures from the military for more control, from business for more autonomy or more power to do its own controlling. Within

the government there was no overall coordination; the administration of such controls as existed were splintered among the various ministries, each jealous of its own prerogatives. The economy was partly controlled, partly free.[47]

Demand for unified, direct controls grew, especially among the military as the ineffectiveness of the attempt to direct the wartime economy without sacrificing business autonomy became increasingly evident. The advent of the government led by General Hideki Tojo brought about sweeping changes in governmental organization, including the abolition of the Ministry of Commerce and Industry and, in its place, the organization of the Munitions Ministry, headed, however, by Nobusuke Kishi, one of the most loyal Commerce and Industry officials. The function of the new Munitions Ministry was to plan and administer all the controls that had so far been implemented by different economic ministries. The result, however, was far from satisfactory. However impressive the ideological veil of collectivism or the organizational framework for coordinated controls, competition and rivalry continued to prevail among the government bureaucracies, the *zaibatsu* combines, and smaller firms alike. As Cohen pointed out, "The theory was good. In practice, it can be categorically stated that the desired unification was never achieved. The services continued to operate independently, some control associations continued to administer allocations and priorities, an adjustment between orders and supplies was never achieved, production was consistently overestimated, and the special priorities were never observed."[48]

AMERICAN ATTITUDES AND PRESURRENDER PLANNING

Perhaps the most important legacy of the German and Japanese use of cartels as a mechanism of mobilization and procurement was the influence exerted on American attitudes. By the late 1930s an antitrust revival had begun in the United States. The NIRA experiment with cartelization as a means of economic recovery having died at the hands of the Supreme Court,[49] President Roosevelt's newly appointed head of the Antitrust Division of the Department of Justice, Thurman Arnold, had begun to cultivate political support and resources for the division and to bring new life to antitrust enforcement.[50] The identification of cartels and monopoly with the menace of fascism fueled these efforts. Arnold was among the first to stress the need for effective antitrust enforcement at home in light of the German experience. "The inevitable end of industrial control by private combinations, cartels and trade associations," he wrote in 1940 "is illustrated by Germany today." In Germany, he continued, arbitrary power without control and regimentation without leadership" created a vacuum and "Hitler leaped into power." "Had it not been Hitler," Arnold added, "it would have been someone else."[51]

Once the United States had entered the war, the rhetoric became even more strident. Books like *Master Plan: The Story of Industrial Offensive* by Joseph Borkin and Charles Welsh, published in 1943 (with an introduction by Thurman Arnold), contributed to the widening view that cartels and industrial concentration were intrinsic to German fascism and vital to Germany's capacity for military aggression. Perceptions hardened. In 1945 Ben W. Lewis, an Oberlin economist and former chief of an advisory staff to the Office of Alien Property Custodian, expressed the prevailing view: "Cartels and combines have been the spearhead of German aggression both prior to and since August 1939; they have constituted the meshwork of the iron net that has bound to slavery all industry in [German] occupied Europe. To stamp out Nazism and to prevent its resurrection it will be necessary to free the world of the possibility that these devices shall ever again be available to the German people."[52]

The characterization of private economic concentration as both an economic and political evil became for many an article of faith. Preservation of competitive economic markets was in turn increasingly identified as a pillar of political democracy. By the end of the war, in hindsight, it seems almost unthinkable not to have given industrial deconcentration, the dismantling of cartels and cartel organizations, as well as the enactment of permanent antitrust legislation high priority in the American efforts to "demilitarize" and "democratize" postwar Germany and Japan. Nevertheless, the issue was not settled until late in the war and might not have been resolved in favor of a strong deconcentration effort and permanent antitrust legislation had it not been for the influence of a small group of antitrust economists who were working to create a postwar international antitrust policy.

A 1941 Temporary National Economic Committee (TNEC) study of German cartels and concentration[53] had also identified the "excessive" concentration of the German economy and its cartelization. The author, Louis Demeratsky, chief of the European Unit of the Commerce Department's Bureau of Foreign and Domestic Commerce, was careful not to overstate the linkage with German fascism. As the war in Europe progressed, however, those planning for an occupation of Germany as well as postwar U.S. international economic policy increasingly joined proposals for an international antitrust policy with the need to eliminate German cartels and to dismantle Krupp, I. G. Farben, and other German industrial giants as causal agents of German aggression.[54] In late summer 1944 addressing the issue was the State Department's special advisory Committee on Private Monopolies and Cartels, which had been organized under the interdepartmental Executive Committee on Foreign Economic Policy and included among its most active members Harvard economist Edward S. Mason as deputy chair, Robert P. Terrill, executive secretary, and Corwin D. Edwards, Northwestern University economist and chair of the Policy Planning Board for the Antitrust Division of the U.S. Department of Justice. Their primary goal was to draft what eventually emerged as the Havana Charter and its provisions against restrictive practices.[55] In September 1944 the committee members reviewed an unsigned staff report "The Relation between Aggression and Business Structure," which asserted that "the vast increase in the scope of monopolistic combines and the increased relative importance of heavy industry" prior to the rise of National Socialism and the war "logically suggest" that the "expansionist tendencies of German industry have found their clearest expression in the policies of the Nazi government."[56] Commenting on the memo, Demeratsky criticized the analysis as extreme. In his view the report "exaggerates the part played by big business in [German] foreign policy."[57]

As Edwards and his colleagues worked to create the foundations for what would in effect have been a global extension of American antitrust policy to prevent the postwar reemergence of international cartels, they avoided the exaggerations Demeratsky warned against. Although willing to welcome to their cause allies who portrayed cartels in terms of a "German menace," they also argued for an international antitrust policy as an essential component of a liberal postwar international trade order. They viewed competition in positive terms as a precondition for economic efficiency, growth, and prosperity. They supported decartelization and deconcentration as a fundamental element of American policy for occupied Germany and ultimately also for Japan as steps toward their broader objective. In a speech to the Consumer's Union in June 1944,[58] Edwards outlined the case for a postwar policy to eliminate international cartels, noting differences in prevailing British and French views and the consequent problems such a program would be apt to encounter. He noted Germany only in passing and made no mention of Japan.

By September the president was convinced. In a well-publicized letter of September 6, 1944, to Secretary of State Cordell Hull, the president articulated the underlying premises of U.S. policy toward Germany and the directions of American postwar international economic policy: "The history of the use of the I. G. Farben trust by the Nazis reads like a detective story. The defeat of the Nazi armies will have to be followed by the eradication of these weapons of economic warfare. But more than the elimination of the political activities of German cartels will be required. Cartel practices which restrict the free flow of goods in foreign commerce will have to be curbed."[59]

After considerable debate and much controversy over how industrially punitive U.S. occupation policy toward Germany would be,[60] by May 1945 a consensus of sorts had been reached and a policy statement for the military commander of the U.S. occupation forces in Germany in the form of a Joint Chiefs of Staff directive (JCS/1067) had been completed.[61] As determined a half a year earlier, JCS/1067 included the mandates of paragraph 5, that "no action will be taken in execution of the reparations program or otherwise which would tend to support basic living conditions in Germany on a higher level than that existing in any of the neighboring countries," and of part II, that "no steps will be taken, a) leading toward the economic rehabilitation of Germany or, b) designed to maintain or strengthen the German economy" except as necessary to carry out stated economic objectives that included "industrial disarmament" in addition to measures to prevent starvation or "such disease and unrest as would endanger [U.S. occupation] forces." The directive separately instructed the commander in chief to take measures to ensure the decartelization and deconcentration of German industry.

Three months later, on August 2, 1945, at Potsdam, President Roosevelt, Chairman Stalin, and Prime Minister Attlee agreed to a common statement of occupation objectives. The protocol did not repeat the JCS directive's prohibition against the measures designed to assist German economic recovery but did provide for German "industrial disarmament" and, needless to say, the decentralization of the German economy "for the purpose of eliminating the present excessive concentration of economic power as exemplified in particular by cartels, syndicates, trusts and other monopolistic arrangements."[62] As German economic recovery became a central issue for U.S. policy, deconcentration also became a subject of considerable controversy. At the outset of occupation, however, no one disagreed that deconcentration and decartelization should be among the primary American aims.

Agreement on the issue of deconcentration with respect to U.S. policy toward Germany was not duplicated in the case of Japan. Deconcentration became official policy for Japan only after intense debate within the Department of State.[63] Opposing the policy was the group of advisors with the greatest claim to expertise on Japan. By 1944 they were led by Joseph C. Grew,[64] U.S. ambassador to Japan from 1932 until the official rupture of U.S. relations with Japan following the attack on Pearl Harbor, and Eugene Dooman, who had served under Grew as embassy counselor for four years before the war. After internment for seven months in Tokyo, Grew, Dooman, and Robert A. Fearey, Grew's young private secretary, returned to Washington. By 1944 Grew and Dooman had together become leading players within the State Department in the formulation of postwar U.S. policy toward Japan. Grew replaced Stanley Hornbeck as director of the Office of Far Eastern Affairs.

Dooman along with Fearey and Earle Dickover, a former first secretary from the Tokyo embassy, were appointed members of the Inter-Divisional Area Committees on the Far East (IDACFE), the State Department's presurrender planning group for Japan. By the end of the year, Grew had become undersecretary of state, the second-highest position in the department (a post he had held in the mid 1920s).

Responding to the proposed inclusion of structural economic reforms as a component of U.S. policy for occupied Japan and mindful of the thrust of some of the early plans for Germany, the Japan specialists feared a retributive destruction of Japanese industrial capacity. They also rejected the view that Japanese industrialists had been in partnership with the military in Japan's preparations for and pursuit of the war. A June 1944 memo[65] from Hugh Borton, a young historian who had been one of the first of the small group of Japanese specialists to join the Special Research Division of the State Department (reorganized in 1943 as the IDACFE), expressed the consensus of the specialists on Japan that, whether or not accurate in the case of Germany, the premise of military-industrialist collusion as an underlying feature of fascism and cause of military aggression did not apply to Japan. The United States, Borton recommended, should "create internal conditions favorable to democracy." With this aim, "Japan should be permitted as soon as possible to resume international trade." He added that in the process of such reforms, the United States should encourage liberal forces within Japan, which, he added, included "a considerable sprinkling of business leaders whose prosperity was based on world trade rather than the greater East Asia prosperity sphere."[66]

Borton's memo echoed Grew's experience as ambassador in Tokyo in the 1930s. Grew had arrived in Japan on June 6, 1932, three months after the assassination of Takuma Dan, the Mitsui Company's chief director, by ultranationalist fanatics and less than a month after the fatal attack on Prime Minister Tsuyoshi Inukai by a similarly inspired band of naval officers. Grew had thus personally observed the hostility of ultranationalist military groups and bureaucrats toward the *zaibatsu* and Japan's business elite. He was also acutely aware that Japan's financial and commercial establishment had initially resisted, often at personal risk, the "tidal wave of insane military megalomania and expansionist ambition."[67] To be sure, as a member of Boston's social elite, he may have identified with the business establishment and perhaps was overly sanguine about how representative or committed those he knew were to "internationalist" values as commercial and financial conglomerates increasingly cooperated in the expansion of Japan's Greater East Asia Co-prosperity Sphere. But, as Grew had witnessed, they had joined the effort at the end, not the beginning, of the parade toward war and defeat. In his view, Japan's strongest business leaders, like other liberals, were "power-less to resist" the military and were "cajoled, bribed, or blackmailed" into coop-eration.[68] Grew, who had spent more than eight years as a diplomat before and during World War I in Berlin and was counselor and chargé d'affaires of the U.S. embassy in Vienna at the time of U.S. entry into the war in 1917,[69] at least perceived that Japan was not Nazi Germany. The only parallel he observed was with German militarism prior to World War I.[70]

To others Japan's industrial structure was much less benign. Especially those who held distinctly Marxist views of Japan drew their own, ideologi-cally correct parallels between the German and the Japanese experiences. No one was more committed, prolific, or critical of Grew and the *zaibatsu* and their influence than T. A. ("Art") Bisson.[71] As a young Presbyterian mission-ary teaching in a middle school for two years in Anhwei Province and at Yenching University for a year in Beijing in the mid 1920s, Bisson connected with the student movement and Chinese nationalism. He returned to the United States in 1928 and began a doctoral degree program in Chinese stud-ies at Columbia. In 1929 he joined the research staff of the Foreign Policy Association, a nonprofit educational and research organization. In the 1930s Bisson became actively associated with Philip Jaffe, managing editor of *China Today,* an official publication of the American Friends of the Chinese People. By 1937 Bisson had also become an editor and frequent contributor to *Amerasia,* a related publication. *China Today* and *Amerasia* were "decidedly left-wing" if not actually controlled by the U.S. Communist Party.[72] They also had offices in close proximity to and interaction with the Institute of Public Affairs,[73] for whose periodical, *Pacific Affairs,* Bisson was to become a regu-lar contributor. In June 1937 Bisson had returned to China with Jaffe. Along with Owen Lattimore, the editor of *Pacific Affairs,* they visited Yenan. The three spent four days in discussions with Mao Zedong, Zhou EnLai, and other Communist leaders.[74] Bisson, caught up in controversy over an article com-paring Mao's movement favorably with the Nationalists[75] and at odds with the prevailing American views on China, devoted his attention thereafter to Japan and the role of the *zaibatsu* in Japan's war effort. In a series of articles in *Amerasia* and *Pacific Affairs* as well as an influential book, *Japan's War Economy* (published in 1945 by the Institute of Pacific Affairs; distributed by the Macmillan Company), Bisson detailed Japan's wartime industrial poli-cies, emphasizing the role of the state and the *zaibatsu* in the mobilization of Japanese industry for war. Between 1943 and 1945, Bisson authored at least five articles for *Pacific Affairs* in which he held the *zaibatsu* equally responsi-ble with the military for Japan's aggressive, "fascist" state.[76] Like those who emphasized the role of cartels and concentration in Germany's successful preparation for war, Bisson viewed the *zaibatsu* as vital partners in Japanese military aggression and the forging of Japanese "fascist-militarist" regime.[77] In the *New Republic* issue of August 27, 1945, in which the editors, skeptical of Grew's views on Japan, separately praised Acheson's replacement of Grew as undersecretary of state, Bisson emphasized Japan's "Imperial clique" and the *zaibatsu*, who were, in Bisson's words, "responsible equally with the militarists" for the war.[78] For those who held similar views, *zaibatsu* dissolution was essential to any attempt to reform Japan and create a democratic Japan. Edwin O. Reischauer could well have had Bisson in mind when he wrote,

> Curiously, the American authorities held to the Marxist interpretation that the real villain behind Japan's imperialism had been the excessive concentration of industrial wealth and power in the hands of the *zaibatsu*, which was thought to have necessitated an aggressive foreign policy. Although Japan's prewar history scarcely bears out this theory, it led to a remarkable display of socialist zeal on the part of MacArthur and his staff.[79]

Bisson's influence is difficult to gauge. He took active part in the occupation with various assignments in Government Section. But he remained only a marginal participant in the reforms. Any part he may have played in the eventual *zaibatsu* dissolution effort was minor at most. He is best remembered for his 1954 study of *zaibatsu* dissolution,[80] which remains the leading study in English. Whether his wartime writings were widely read or had any influence on those who were planning for the occupation is even more difficult to determine. What is important—and underlies the emphasis on Bisson and his views here—is that he represented the extreme end of a spectrum of knowledgeable and articulate members of the American intellectual community whose views, although not as far to the left as Bisson's, did count. They viewed the *zaibatsu* primarily in political rather than economic terms. They condemned the *zaibatsu* like other concentrations of corporate wealth as antithetical to the development and growth of democratic institutions. They believed that *zaibatsu* dissolution like German deconcentration was an essential component of any effort to create democratic institutions in Japan. They were hostile to private but not public monopoly. They rejected state planning and controls only if not carried out within a "democratic" political structure. However, neither those Japan specialists who may have sided with Bisson or with Grew were to play a decisive role in presurrender planning. That honor belongs to the economists.

The Committee on Private Monopolies and Cartels had ignored Japan completely throughout the discussions of postwar economic policy. Of a total